POISON!

DEADLY FiSH

Shane McFee

Published in 2008 by The Rosen Publishing Group, Inc.
29 East 21st Street, New York, NY 10010

Copyright © 2008 by The Rosen Publishing Group, Inc.

First Edition

Editor: Jennifer Way
Book Design: Kate Laczynski
Photo Researcher: Nicole Pristash

Photo Credits: Cover, p. 1 © Kevin Schafer/Getty Images; pp. 5, 7, 9, 11, 15, 17, 21 © Shutterstock.com; pp. 13, 17 (inset), 19 © SuperStock, Inc.

Library of Congress Cataloging-in-Publication Data

McFee, Shane.
  Deadly fish / Shane McFee. — 1st ed.
      p. cm. — (Poison!)
  Includes index.
  ISBN-13: 978-1-4042-3798-8 (library binding)
  ISBN-10: 1-4042-3798-4 (library binding)
  1. Poisonous fishes—Juvenile literature. I. Title.
  QL618.7.M34 2008
  597.16'5—dc22
                                        2006102910

Manufactured in the United States of America

CONTENTS

DEADLY FISH!

Did you know that some **species** of fish are deadly? When you think of deadly fish, you may think of sharks. However, there are many dangerous fish that are much smaller than sharks. These fish have poisonous **venom** that they use for hunting and **defense**.

There are more than 24,600 different species of fish in the world. Scientists believe that more than 1,200 of these species are venomous. Stargazers, lionfish, puffer fish, and stonefish are some of the most venomous fish in the world. This book will tell you more about them.

This is a lionfish, a venomous fish that can be found in warm ocean waters throughout most of the world. There are more species of venomous fish than venomous snakes in the world!

WHAT ARE DEADLY FISH?

Many people think that any animal that spends its life in the water is a fish. This is not true. For example, dolphins live in the water, and they are not fish. Dolphins breathe air above the water.

Unlike dolphins, most fish are **cold blooded**. Fish breathe underwater with gills. Gills are the organs, or body parts, that fish use for breathing instead of lungs.

Most venomous fish have **spines**. These spines are sharp, like needles are. The spines are used to **inject** venom into an animal the same way a doctor's needle gives you a shot.

The sharp spines on this porcupine fish can give nasty stings! This fish got its name because its spines look like the spines on a porcupine.

COLOR AND CAMOUFLAGE

The way that fish look can help them **survive**. Some venomous fish have bright colors that warn other animals to keep away. Lionfish usually have bright colors and stripes. This warns other animals to leave the lionfish alone. The lionfish can then stay safe without having to use its poison to defend itself.

Other venomous fish use **camouflage**. Stonefish are usually brown. The rocks at the bottom of the ocean are also brown. The stonefish's **prey** will think it is a rock and swim right up to it only to get eaten! The stonefish's **predators** will also think it is a rock and leave it alone.

It might take you a while to see the stonefish in this picture. Its bumpy skin camouflages it so that it looks like the rocks around it.

VENOM

Some deadly fish use their venom only for defense. However, it is hard for them to attack with their spines. The lionfish can use its venom only if something runs into its spines.

The venom of these deadly fish is very powerful. It defends the fish from very large animals. The venom of deadly fish is very dangerous to people.

Some venom attacks the **nervous system**. This is the system in the body that connects the brain to the rest of the body. Attacking the nervous system causes **paralysis** and even death.

A sting from a lionfish, like the one shown here, might cause pain and swelling. A really bad sting can cause the skin around the wound to turn black and fall off!

STARGAZERS

Stargazers have eyes on the top of their head. This makes them look like they are looking up toward the sky. This is how they got their name.

Stargazers bury themselves in the sand to hide from predators. They also do this so they can surprise their prey. Some stargazers have a worm-shaped fold near their mouth. An unlucky fish will mistake this fold for food and get too close to the stargazer and end up as the stargazer's food!

Stargazers have two venomous spines. They also have special organs near their eyes that make electric shocks. These shocks are very powerful under water.

LiONFiSH

The lionfish has about 12 venomous spines. Sometimes these spines break off and stay in the hurt animal. Even dead lionfish are deadly to something that runs into their spines!

When a lionfish hunts, it corners its prey by spreading out its large fins. Then the lionfish swallows the prey whole.

Lionfish are usually found only in tropical water, which is water that is warm year-round. However, there are now a growing number of them living off the coast of New York.

The lionfish's striped spines are interesting to look at but venomous. Lionfish are sometimes known as turkey fish, dragon fish, or scorpion fish.

PUFFER FISH

You may have seen a puffer fish before. The puffer fish has a very interesting way of defending itself from predators. It puffs itself up by sucking in water. The puffer fish can grow to several times its nonpuffed size. This is often enough to scare away predators that do not already know that this fish is poisonous.

The puffer fish does not have venom. It uses a different kind of poison. The puffer fish has **toxins** in its organs. This means that a puffer fish is dangerous to eat. The toxins in a puffer fish are strong enough to kill most people.

Puffer fish are also called blowfish because of the way they make their body blow up like a balloon (inset). You can eat the puffer fish if it has been prepared carefully. The poisonous organs can be removed.

STONEFISH

The stonefish gets its name because it camouflages itself to look like a rock. It is the most dangerous venomous fish. If a person steps on it, the stonefish will inject its venom into him or her. Unlike most venomous fish, the stonefish can control the amount of venom it injects.

The stonefish's venom is very powerful and dangerous to people. It will cause terrible pain and paralysis. A person who has been poisoned by a stonefish needs to go to a hospital as soon as possible.

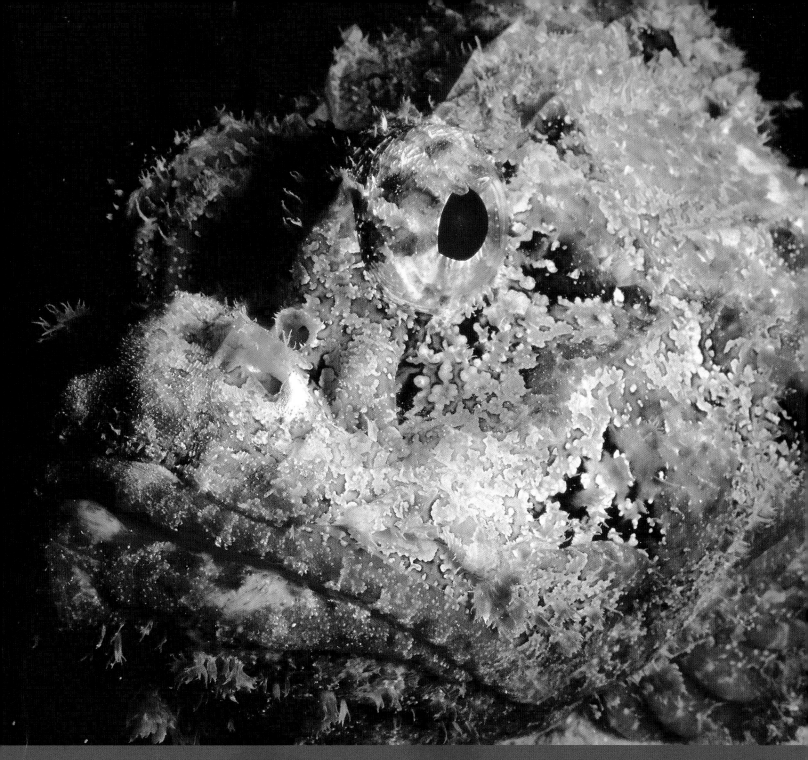

Stonefish live in the tropical waters of the Pacific and Indian oceans. They eat small fish, shrimp, and other shellfish.

AQUARIUMS

Have you ever been to an aquarium? An aquarium is like a zoo for fish. Aquariums are the best and safest places for you to see deadly fish. The people who work at aquariums know how to handle these species safely. Aquariums are also great places for scientists to study deadly fish. We still do not know very much about these animals.

Some people own deadly fish as pets. This is not a good idea for people who do not know very much about these kinds of fish. These fish are very dangerous. Stargazers and stonefish are not friendly. Remember, stargazers can also shock you.

Aquariums are great places to see sea animals up close. You can learn about animals from all around the world without the danger of hurting them or being hurt by them.

WHAT SHOULD YOU DO?

If you are poisoned by a deadly fish, you must go to the hospital. All these fish can be deadly to people. Lionfish poisonings sometimes can be treated by placing the wound in hot water for 30 to 40 minutes. Other kinds of deadly fish poisons may require drugs and other care from a doctor.

Be careful when you swim in tropical places, because this is where most of these types of fish live. Keep in mind that both stonefish and stargazers can be hard to see. Hopefully the only way you will see these deadly fish is through the glass of an aquarium!

GLOSSARY

camouflage (KA-muh-flahj) A color or shapes that match what is around something and help hide it.

cold blooded (KOHLD BLUH-did) Having a body heat that changes with the surrounding heat.

defense (dih-FENS) Something a living thing does that helps keep it safe.

inject (in-JEKT) To force something into the body.

nervous system (NER-vus SIS-tum) A system of nerve fibers in people and animals.

paralysis (puh-RA-luh-sus) Loss of feeling or movement in a part of the body.

predators (PREH-duh-terz) Animals that kill other animals for food.

prey (PRAY) An animal that is hunted by another animal for food.

species (SPEE-sheez) One kind of living thing. All people are one species.

spines (SPYNZ) Parts of an animal that stick out.

survive (sur-VYV) To live longer than, to stay alive.

toxins (TOK-sinz) Poisons made by a plant or an animal that hurt another plant or animal.

venom (VEH-num) A poison passed by one animal into another.

INDEX

WEB SITES

Due to the changing nature of Internet links, PowerKids Press has developed an online list of Web sites related to the subject of this book. This site is updated regularly. Please use this link to access the list:
www.powerkidslinks.com/poi/dfish/